A NEW COMPANION

TO ADVENT &
CHRISTMASTIDE

*All booklets are published thanks to the
generous support of the members of the
Catholic Truth Society*

CATHOLIC TRUTH SOCIETY
PUBLISHERS TO THE HOLY SEE

2

CONTENTS

BEHOLD HE IS COMING

"Behold, He is coming!" It is the coming of the Word of God, the Word made flesh, which we celebrate, commemorate and anticipate in the seasons of Advent and Christmas. We celebrate Him, because He is coming to us now; we commemorate Him because He came once long ago in Bethlehem; we anticipate Him because His coming will eventually be made manifest in glory.

What moods should prevail, what attitude should we take before that Coming, past, present and yet to come? We are glad and grateful when we think of the past, determined to reform our lives and be truly loving when we receive Him really present, reverent and even fearful in the face of the future. The liturgy and the traditional activities of this season reflect all these moods, intertwined and interactive, so that at the same time we can be penitent and joyful, awe-struck and confident, remorseful and ebullient.

Christmas past

When we reflect on Christmas past, we remember the actual historical events of the birth of Our Saviour. It was in a particular place, which some of us have visited, at a particular date, which we can calculate to within a year or so, that a particular woman, a fellow human creature, to whom we are all related, however distantly, gave birth to the Son of God. We read and re-read the ancient story, in St Matthew (1:18-2:23) and St Luke (1:5-2:52), and we ponder on the glorious meditation which St John (1:1-18) wrote on the meaning of what happened: God and Man are united, the creator and the creature made one. Nothing more important has ever happened or could happen. We are not on our own, trying to swim through the universe unaided: for God is with us, He is on our side; He shares our life so that we can share His. For that reason we rejoice, and express our joy in festivity and jollity.

Christmas present

When we reflect on Christmas present, we realise that this Christ who came long ago is with us now, truly present in the Sacrament of the Altar. At every moment of the day or night, somewhere in the world the Mass is being celebrated, and He comes again. In the Tabernacle He resides as the living heart of the parish. As we receive Him in Holy Communion we become, each of us, members of His Body, so that the Church throughout the world becomes "one body, one spirit in Christ". The Eucharist is formed by the Church; the Church is formed by the Eucharist, so that Christ comes to us in each other, in the Church as a whole, precisely because in the Sacrament He comes into our innermost being, giving life and love. And so we express this in our mutual charity, to love one another as He loves us. To celebrate that presence we give presents to each other, gifts to those we know and love, to those we have failed to love enough, to those we do not know but are desperately in need of our love.

Judgment yet to come

When we reflect on Christmas yet to come, we cannot fail to be anxious and fearful, no matter how joyful and confident we are of His love, when we remember that at some date, maybe soon, maybe in millions of years' time, human history will be wound up, and a reckoning made of all that we have done, all that we have failed to do. "For if you should mark our iniquities, Lord who could endure it?" (*Ps* 129:3) What terrible things we poor human creatures have done to each other, to the world God gave us, to the other creatures He made for our amusement! When the books are opened, and Our Lord comes as judge, how can any of us dare to claim any rights against Him? The judgment He makes is just, for it depends entirely on how we have fulfilled His commandment to love one another, as He loves us (*Mt* 25:1-46). But His judgment is loving and merciful, for all who acknowledge their guilt and fly to Him for forgiveness will surely be welcomed. That is why part of our Advent must be examination of conscience, confession and absolution; and a mood of penitence and self-denial that befits our realisation that we have failed to live in love in His presence.

In the tradition of the Church the actual season of Advent was a time of penance, when with drab vestments the liturgy reflected on our need for God's healing love; a time for confession and for simple living, cutting down on our excess of food and drink and entertainment to make space in our lives for the love of God and neighbour. It lasts, at the very most, twenty-eight days: it is followed by forty days of rejoicing! For twelve days, until the great and significant feast of Epiphany on the 6th of January, the Church went wild with joy, an unbroken time of gladness and charity; then until Candlemas the celebration continued, though on a more reasonable scale, as daily work began again, and the normal rhythm of life was restored to some extent. All that seems to have been swept away under the pressures of conformity to the secular world around us, but we should understand what these seasons once were: penance followed by rejoicing, and, as always, the Church offers us a season of rejoicing which is much longer than that of penitence!

The Advent Season

A call to hope

The season of advent is one of the most beautiful of the Church's liturgical year. As the weather grows colder and the days shorten, the prayers and readings of this holy season inspire us with hope, encouraging us to look forward in joyful expectation to the coming of the 'Sun of Justice', Jesus Christ. 'The people who walked in darkness have seen a great light…' (*Is* 9:2)

Sadly, for so many who live in our secularised world, Advent has no meaning. Even for Catholics, it is so easy to pass the whole of December in a frantic preparation for Christmas. So many cards to post, presents to buy, preparations to make, meals to be cooked and eaten - and yet the Church invites us to spends these weeks in a very different spirit. Advent (from the Latin, *Adventus*) means 'coming'. During this season we look forward to the coming of Jesus Christ and we practise that most difficult and necessary of virtues - patience. We also exercise the theological virtue of HOPE - a faith-filled trust in God's promises. Pondering the marvellous works of God in the Old Testament, we long to see them fulfilled in the wonder of the Incarnation, and we also look forward to the final coming of Christ, his coming at the end of time, when those promises will be definitively fulfilled, and God will make all things new.

The spirit of Advent

The season of Advent falls into two halves: in the first part (and especially on the First Sunday) we look forward with hope to the Second Coming of Christ at the end of the world. In the second part, as the feast of Christmas draws nearer, we turn our minds to Bethlehem, and to the first coming of Christ among us, made flesh in the womb of Mary.

St Bernard of Clairvaux, in a famous sermon on Advent, speaks of a 'third coming' of Christ, between his birth at Bethlehem and the Second Coming at the end of time. This third coming is the coming of Christ into our mind and hearts, made possible when we hear the word of God, and meditate upon it, and when we receive the sacraments which make our faith grow strong. 'In short' says St Bernard 'The first coming was in flesh and in weakness, this intermediary coming is in the spirit and in power, the last coming will be in glory and majesty. This intermediary coming is like a road leading from the first to the last coming. In the first coming Christ was our redemption, in the last he will appear as our life, in this intermediary coming he is our rest and consolation'.

Advent is the perfect time to meditate on this 'third coming' of Christ into our lives. How sad if we fail to welcome him, if we grow so busy in our preparations for Christmas that we neglect the very person we are supposed to be celebrating! Let us force ourselves to put aside a little space for prayer each day, to really learn the lesson of the Advent scriptures (some of the most lovely of the Church's year), and to make a home in our hearts for Christ the Lord.

The Advent Liturgy

Historically, Advent is not one of the oldest seasons of the liturgical year. It originated, probably, about the Sixth or Seventh Century. Often beginning shortly after the feast of St Martin (11 November) it was known in the Middle Ages as 'St Martin's Lent', and indeed it does share many of the characteristics of the Lenten season. The colour of the vestments is purple, the 'Gloria' is omitted, and Advent helps us prepare spiritually for Christmas in much the same way as Lent prepares us for Easter. Nevertheless, Advent has a special character all of its own. Our focus is not so much on penance for our sins as on waiting, patiently, for the fulfilment of the Lord's promises, acknowledging as we do so that our world is still very much wounded by sin and in need of God's redemption.

As we noted above, purple vestments are worn during Advent, because purple is the colour of waiting. However, in many churches, on the Third Sunday of Advent (known as *Gaudete* or 'rejoicing' Sunday), pink or rose-coloured vestments are worn, signifying that we have reached the half-way point in the Advent journey, and a sign that the light of Christmas will shortly dawn upon us. The 'Gloria' is not sung because it is in origin a Christmas song - sung by the angels over Bethlehem. We will sing it again at Midnight Mass, the first Mass of the Nativity.

Advent wreath

In many churches it is now the custom to have an 'Advent Wreath' placed somewhere near the sanctuary. It consists of a circle of evergreen foliage (symbol of eternity) in which are placed five candles, which correspond to the colour of the vestments - three purple, one pink and one (in the centre) which is white. The wreath is blessed on the First Sunday of Advent and the candles are gradually lighted Sunday by Sunday, providing a simple visible reminder of the passing of the weeks of Advent, while the growing light of the candles anticipates the joyful season of Christmas when the final, white candle, will be lighted.

Advent calendar

In many homes, of course, it is the custom to have an 'Advent Calendar'. The children of the house open a different window each day, ending with the opening of the last window on Christmas Eve. Like so much else in the Western world, this old practice has been commercialised in recent times, with calendars featuring cartoon characters and film stars, and the windows concealing chocolates and other treats! Try and find a proper Christian Advent calendar which focuses on the real meaning of the season. Your children will still enjoy opening the window each day, and it will be a daily reminder to them of the importance of our faith and the reason for our joy at Christmas.

PRAYING IN THE SEASON OF ADVENT

Help in the Scriptures

Here we will suggest a few brief thoughts to inspire you in your prayer during advent, drawing especially on the Sunday liturgy. You will notice that many of the Old Testament readings, especially on weekdays, are taken from the prophet Isaiah. He is, in a special way the 'spokesman' of the Advent season. His voice is always heard on the First Sunday of Advent, and many of his prophecies were fulfilled at Christ's birth at Bethlehem (most obviously the prophecy in *Isaiah* 7:14 - 'Behold a virgin will conceive and bear a son'). You might like to make the *Book of Isaiah* a feature of your Advent reading: alternatively you could follow the pattern of the weekday readings as they appear in the Lectionary. You will see that the First Reading always contains a prophecy which is fulfilled in the Gospel. Thus Christ came to fulfil the whole of the Old Testament.

Try too to find a little time during advent for *silence*. This is the most precious of commodities, especially in the run-up to Christmas, but it is also essential to real growth in the spirit. It was in the silence of the night that Christ was born in Bethlehem, and it is only in the silence of our hearts that he can be born again in our world today.

The First Sunday of Advent

The three year cycle of readings continues during Advent, but no matter which year we are in, we can be sure that the scriptures today will be focussed on the Second Coming and the end of the world.

This can be a challenging subject for Christians today! On the one hand, in our troubled times, we can identify with the scenarios the readings conjure up (wars, revolutions, disasters), yet we can find it very hard to imagine the Second Coming as a real event, still harder to 'long for' the end of time as the liturgy encourages us to do. Maybe the problem lies in part in our secularised world - we are made to feel that our faith, if acceptable at all, is purely private, with no social consequences. The liturgy today (like that of last Sunday, the Feast of Christ the King) reminds us that Christ is no marginal figure in history. He is the Son of God, who created and redeemed the world, and at the end of time all humanity will acknowledge him, believers and non-believers alike. As Christians, therefore, our faith can NEVER be a purely private affair - it inspires us to go out and make Christ known, and to play some small part in preparing for the coming of his Kingdom, even here and now in our time.

'It is not enough for us, then, to be content with his first coming: we must wait in hope of his second coming. What we said at his first coming 'Blessed is he who comes in the name of the Lord' we shall repeat at his last coming. Running out with the angels to meet the Master, we shall cry out in adoration 'Blessed is he who comes in the name of the Lord!' (*St Cyril of Jerusalem*).

The Second Sunday of Advent

Today, John the Baptist makes his appearance. He, too, can be a challenging and 'uncomfortable' figure. Standing as he does at the very edge of the New Testament, he is both the last of the Old Testament prophets and one of the first of the Christian martyrs. Neither prophets nor martyrs are very 'comfortable' figures, especially if our faith is a little less fervent than it might be! Crying aloud in the desert, clothed in camel skin and living off locusts, John seems a reproach to the feasting, partying and self-indulgence that can overtake us during this time of year. Yes, it is only right to celebrate the birth of Jesus, but John reminds us that first we must do a little self-examination and soul-searching too. We need to have the humility to acknowledge our sinfulness, our failings and our frailty - and to acknowledge our NEED of a Saviour. We too need to accompany John into the desert, and there come face to face with God.

'As God sees the world tottering to ruin because of fear he acts unceasingly to bring it back by love, invite it by grace, to hold it by charity and clasp it firmly with affection'. (*St Peter Chrysologus*).

The Third Sunday of Advent

Today is often called *Gaudete*, or 'rejoicing' Sunday. The name comes from the Entrance Antiphon to the Mass:

'Rejoice in the Lord always: again I say rejoice! The Lord is near.'

The Lord is near! Two weeks of our Advent preparation have already passed - today the priest may wear pink vestments, the third candle on the Advent Wreath is lit, and during the next few days the Church's liturgy will turn more attentively to the coming of the Lord at Bethlehem.

But what about us? Half of Advent is already gone. Have we made any spiritual progress, given any more time to prayer, are we really any better prepared to greet the birth of Jesus on Christmas Day? Once again today, the Gospel reading focuses on John the Baptist, the faithful witness, challenging us too to 'prepare the way of the Lord' and to make a home for him in our hearts.

'What does "to prepare the way" mean, except to pray as you ought, to be humble minded? Take an example of humility from John himself. He is thought to be the Christ, but he says he is not what people think. He knew where his salvation lay. He understood that he was a lamp, and he was afraid of being quenched by the wind of pride.' (*St Augustine*).

The Fourth Sunday of Advent

Now we are very close to Christmas. The great feast might even be tomorrow, and it cannot be more than a week away. As we draw nearer to the birth of Jesus, the Gospel today introduces us to Mary, not only the Mother of God, but his most faithful follower.

The whole of advent is very much a 'Marian' season. We await, along with Mary, the birth of her divine Son. We try hard to practise her virtues of patience, humility and generosity before God. Why not try to pray the rosary during these next days, especially the Five Joyful Mysteries? Ask Our Lady to pray for you, to make you more worthy to celebrate joyfully the birth of our Redeemer: above all try to imitate the openness she showed towards God: 'I am the handmaid of the Lord - be it done unto me according to your word'.

'God gave to Mary his Son, the only begotten of his heart, equal to himself, whom he loved as himself. From Mary he fashioned himself a Son, not another one but the same, so that by nature there would be one and the same Son both of God and of Mary. Every nature is created by God, and God is born of Mary. God created all things and Mary gave birth to God. God himself, who made all things, made himself from Mary. In this way he remade all that he had made. He who was able to make all things out of nothing, when they had been defaced would not remake them without Mary's help.' (*St Anselm*).

The 'O' Antiphons

These antiphons are used between 17 December and 23 December at Vespers, or Evening Prayer, which forms part of the Divine Office (or the 'Prayer of the Church'). If you are not able to attend the Divine Office you might at least like to recite these antiphons as part of your personal prayer on these days. They are some of the most beautiful compositions in the Church's liturgy, drawn from many places in scripture and illustrating the role of Christ as our Redeemer.

The 'O' Antiphons have been in use since the Middle Ages. In monasteries, 17 December, when the antiphons begin, is often treated a sort of feast day, when the community might be treated to a special meal or a glass of wine. Sometimes, members of the community take it in turns to begin the antiphons, depending on their role in the monastery. For example, the antiphon beginning '*O Radix*' (O Root of Jesse) might be sung by a gardener: '*O Clavis*' (O Key of David) by the gatekeeper, ands so on.

17 December: '*O Sapientia*'
O Wisdom, you come forth from the mouth of the Most High. You fill the universe and hold all things together in a strong yet gentle manner. O come to teach us the way of truth.

18 December: 'O Adonai'

O Adonai and leader of Israel, you appeared to Moses in a burning bush and you gave us the Law on Sinai. O come and save us with your mighty power.

19 December: 'O Radix Jesse'

O Root of Jesse, you stand as a signal for the nations: kings fall silent before you whom the peoples acclaim. O come and deliver us, and do not delay.

20 December: 'O Clavis David'

O Key of David and sceptre of Israel, what you open no one can close again; what you close no one can open. O come to lead the captive from prison: free those who sit in darkness and in the shadow of death.

21 December: 'O Oriens'

O Rising Sun, you are the splendour of eternal light and the sun of justice. O come and enlighten those who sit in darkness and in the shadow of death.

22 December: 'O Rex Gentium'

O King whom all the peoples desire, you are the cornerstone which makes all one. O come and save man whom you made from clay.

23 December: 'O Emmanuel'

O Emmanuel, you are our King and Judge, the one whom the peoples await and their Saviour. O come and save us, Lord our God!

SOME ADVENT SAINTS

There are certain saints' days which always fall during Advent. Here are some of the most important ones.

St Francis Xavier - 3 December

Francis Xavier was born in 1506 at Pamplona, in Spain. While studying in Paris he became one of the first followers of St Ignatius Loyola, the founder of the Jesuits. St Ignatius selected Francis for the work of an apostle, sending him out to evangelise the still recently-discovered countries of the East. St Francis travelled across India, Japan and reached the outskirts of China, preaching and baptising thousands of new converts. Worn out by his labours he died in 1552, and is now buried in Goa, where his shrine attracts many pilgrims.

St Francis reminds us of the importance of *making Christ known*. Jesus came as 'a light to the Gentiles' (*Lk* 2:32), and the Saviour of the whole human race. We can never treat our faith as a private possession: it is something to be shared.

St Nicholas - 6 December

The original 'Santa Claus', St Nicholas was Bishop of Myra, in Turkey, during the Fourth Century. He was a great defender of the Catholic Faith, and much loved by his people. One story relates that he once saved three penniless girls from a life of prostitution, by secretly providing them with dowries to get married. Another story says that he saved three small boys who were about to be eaten alive! In these legends of his kindness, we see the origins of the genial figure who is supposed to provide small children with their Christmas presents today.

Perhaps more importantly, St Nicholas was a great defender of Christ's divinity against the heresy of Arius. Arius denied that Christ was God (which would make the celebration of Christmas meaningless!). Let us ask St Nicholas to intercede for us, that our own faith in the truth of the Incarnation may grow stronger.

The Immaculate Conception - 8 December

Today we celebrate the fact that Our Lady was conceived free from all stain of Original Sin, the better to prepare her for becoming the Mother of God.

The name 'Mary' (*Miriam*, in Hebrew) means 'Star of the Sea'. Today we can think of Mary's Immaculate Conception as a star which lights up the darkness of our world, and guides us on our pilgrim way. She also brings with her the promise of the dawn, because soon we shall celebrate Christmas, and the coming of a Saviour for all the world. St Bernard of Clairvaux, in one of his sermons, writes in praise of Mary:

'She, I say, is that clear and shining star, twinkling with brilliance and resplendent with example, set by necessity above the surface of this great and wide sea. And you, whosoever you may be, who know yourself to be there, not walking upon the firm ground but battered to and fro by gales and the storms of this life's ocean, if you will not to be overwhelmed by the tempest, keep your eyes fixed upon this star's clear shining. In danger, in difficulty or in doubt, call on Mary.'

St Lucy - 13 December

St Lucy suffered martyrdom at Syracuse, in Sicily, probably during the persecution of Diocletian (early Fourth Century). It is said that she preferred to die rather than surrender the virginity she had pledged to Christ. One tradition also says that her eyes were plucked out during her martyrdom, for which reason she is specially invoked by those who have problems with their sight.

The name 'Lucy' means 'light' and during these dark winter days, while we are waiting for the coming of the light of Christmas, we take inspiration from all those who, like St Lucy, have gone before us marked with the sign of faith. The Antiphon for Morning Prayer on her feast day gives us Lucy's own words. She says, 'I am the lowly servant of the Lord, who wished only to offer everything to the living God. Now since there is nothing left to be offered, I give myself to him'. Let that be our prayer too.

CHRISTMAS

Origins and history

They tell us that Easter is the most important feast of the Christian year, but instinctively we love Christmas more. Perhaps that is because, in common with the Fathers of the Early Church, we recognize that the Incarnation, the fact that God is made man, is the most important event of all. Actually that should make us lay more stress on the feast of the Annunciation, 25 March, the day when Our Lady conceived. For most of our history in most Christian countries that was kept as the first day of the year, because that was the real beginning of the Incarnation. Moreover, 25 March was also, traditionally, the actual day of the Crucifixion, so that Our Lord's life began and ended on the same day, the burgeoning of spring and new life. That is why His birth is celebrated nine months later, on 25 December, and indeed it appears that in the history of the Church's calendar, the date of Christmas was fixed for precisely that reason, nine months after the earlier feast.

Modern dangers

But midwinter has always been celebrated for its own sake, as nature (in our northern hemisphere) turns from decline to growth, and so the church welcomed customs and traditions designed to celebrate the appearance of new life and light in the still darkness of midwinter. That is why not all of our Christmas customs are particularly Christian, and why it is so easy for the feast of Our Lord's Incarnation to degenerate into a pagan festival of greed. We need to tread carefully between the extremes of secular decadence and sour-faced righteousness. It would be lovely if we could once again keep Advent special, and begin our jollities with a flourish once dark falls on Christmas Eve, but it would be cruel to our children to refuse to allow them to celebrate Christmas with their school-friends in November and early December. How can we preserve something of the magic of Christmas, on the night of 24-25 December, when our children are already bored with Christmas by the middle of December? And how can we keep our jollification for the proper Twelve Days of Christmas, until 6 January, when shops begin the sales on 26 December, all public decorations come down on 1 January and schools start immediately afterwards?

National traditions

Families of European origin have an advantage, because they can make a point of preserving national traditions: the Dutch can leave presents in the children's' shoes on 6 December; the Swedes can light St Lucy's candles on 13 December; the Poles can eat carp and break unleavened bread together while waiting for Midnight Mass; the Ukrainians can keep the whole business till 7 January and have a truly religious festival long after the world has forgotten Christmas! For traditions have been very different in different countries. Tragically in old England most of the genuine traditions have been lost, and we have a mish-mash of pagan superstitions (like the Tree) and American commercialism (like Santa Claus), tempered by the Scottish insistence on celebrating the night of 1 January. This last was instituted in the 19th century because Scots Protestants disapproved of keeping Christmas at all, but their children wanted some sort of winter festival like their English rivals; the result was the invention of "New Year", which was taken up enthusiastically by Communist regimes to do down Christmas. 1 January is certainly a feast-day, originally the Circumcision of Our Lord, now the Motherhood of Our Lady.

What we can do, even now, is to Christianize some of the pagan traditions, and to emphasize some of the Christian customs, and help our children to keep Christmas special even after they have become sick of turkey.

Christmas Crib

The first thing is to make much of the Christmas Crib, that lovely invention of St Francis. In Italy and Austria crib figures of astonishing variety are made and sold in the fairs during Advent, and if you buy just one figure a

year you can eventually build up a family set, to rival the
fantastic cribs of Naples. Alternatively, the family can
make their own figures: carved in wood, or modelled in
clay. As well as the obvious figures of the Holy Family,
the Shepherds, Angels and Magi, all sorts of other
citizens of Bethlehem and their visitors can be added,
with buildings and scenery. There is great scope for
imagination and interest. But it is important that the crib
does not get put together until Christmas Eve, and the
Baby is not placed in the Manger until the family have
returned from Midnight Mass: that way it is new and
exciting on Christmas morning, and Magi can be watched
approaching gradually, day by day, until they too reach
the crib. The saints of the days after Christmas can appear
as well, each on their proper days, with dozens of babies
for the Holy Innocents. Patron saints of members of the
family can creep in as well, until by Twelfth Night the
crib is full and no one has had time to get bored with it.

Christmas decorations

The same can apply to house decorations: if they go up
too early they are dusty and boring long before 25
December. Ideally no decorations should be seen until
after the smaller ones have gone to bed on Christmas Eve,
so that when they wake in the morning the whole house is
transformed. Or at least, the decorating should not begin
until the afternoon of Christmas Eve. Traditionally

decorations were evergreen leafy twigs, the holly and the ivy, gathered on Christmas Eve, and hung around the house: a spring of holly behind every picture, swags of ivy over the doors, the mistletoe hanging from the ceiling lights. All of these have been given Christian meanings, as we sing in various carols, and we should remember these. Whenever we are prickled by the holly, we remember the Crown of Thorns!

Christmas tree

The Tree, too can be given a Christian meaning, for we remember the Tree of Life and the Tree of the Knowledge of Good and Evil, where all our problems began, and the Tree of the Cross where they were solved. On top there should be an angel bringing the Good News, or a Star to summon the Magi. I suppose real candles are no longer possible, but the lights can still remind us of the coming of light into darkness, looking forward to Candlemas and the arrival of the True Light that enlightens all men.

Christmas presents

Christmas presents can be a real problem, as they are often the occasion of unbridled greed and commercialism, yet the whole point is charity and Christian love. The business world survives on lavish over-spending at Christmas; but family life will survive much better without the ensuing credit-card debts. Adults can be expected to understand that we are trying to live within our means, or trying to give more to those that need it most, but we must be careful not to be too mean towards the children: they expect good things, all their school-friends will get good things, and they should not be disappointed. Presents must come with love, because they are an expression of the love we must have for one another. And even the smallest children will understand the need to give to those who have nothing. That of course is one aspect of Christmas which must come early: if we are collecting gifts for those who are really in need, whether in our own country or overseas, they must be ready in time!

The giver of gifts has taken many forms in many countries: for some it is St Nicholas, for others the Befana, for others the Christ Child Himself who comes at night and leaves presents for good children. A spare uncle at Christmas can be dressed up as St Nicholas in a cardboard-and-tinsel mitre and can hand out the presents from below the Tree, while giving a lead to the carol singing.

Christmas Eve

In the Invitatory Antiphon which begins the Divine Office, the Church sings this morning; 'Know today that the Lord will come: in the morning you will see his glory'. Today indeed the Lord will come.

Try to remember the excitement you felt as a child, when Christmas Eve came round. All of us should feel a little of that excitement, as we wait again for the commemoration of Our Lord's birth at Bethlehem. Today, more than any, is a day for waiting, for hope, and for confidence in God.

We know that at the time of the first Christmas, the whole world was filled with expectation, longing for a saviour who could break the old patterns of sin and death. In the Jewish scriptures Isaiah prophesied a time of peace to come: 'The wolf will lie down with the lamb, the panther lie down with the kid: the calf, the lion and the sheep shall abide together, and a little child shall lead them' (*Is* 11:6). Even the pagan poet, Virgil, who lived about this time, wrote of his longings for a new beginning: 'The last age foretold is at hand: a new race is being sent down to the earth from heaven. The flock shall no more fear the fierce lions. The serpent shall be no more: the treacherous plant, which yielded poison, shall grow no more' (*Virgil, Fourth Ecologue*).

Jesus was born to satisfy the hope and desires of all the world. Never let us take the blessings he brought for granted. On this, the last day of Advent, let us pray for a greater appreciation of the gifts of God, for a firmer faith and stronger love.

This evening, turn your thoughts to Joseph and Mary, as they complete the journey they have undertaken in obedience to the Emperor's decree (*Lk* 2:1), and arrive at the little town of Bethlehem. As night draws on they take shelter in the quiet stable, and there await the birth of Jesus.

In your prayers you might like to use this antiphon, which was written in the Middle Ages, '*O Virgo virginum*':

"O Virgin of virgins! How shall this be? For never before was there anyone like you, nor shall there ever be again. O daughters of Jerusalem, why do you look wonderingly at me? The thing you behold is a divine mystery."

When Christmas day arrives

Christmas Day itself is the day on which the lonely can get most depressed, and are most in need of company. That is why giving lavish parties for "the elderly" or "the housebound" a week or so before Christmas may not help as much as providing something on the Day itself. Maybe parishes could arrange a Christmas lunch for those living alone, while still enabling parishioners to keep their own family Christmas in the evening. Actually inviting strangers to share a family Christmas meal must be done with great tact and care, so that the children's Christmas is not spoilt, and the guest is not patronised or made to feel embarrassed. All the same, most families seem to have an unwanted uncle or great-aunt who turns up every Christmas and has to be entertained, which can provide great opportunities for the exercise of patience, tolerance and charity.

How to be happy?

Food and drink play an important part in any celebration, and there should be great opportunities for everyone to be happy. Even the cook should be happy, which is why traditionally a considerable proportion of Christmas fare was prepared days or even weeks before the day. Somehow the set "Christmas dinner" has become so standard that people are frightened to vary it, even when they know that most of the family don't really like it. But why be hidebound by (very recent) custom? It is not actually an article of faith that you have to have a turkey: they do tend to be dry and dull, and far too much is left over so that it comes back cold day after day and you begin to think a turkey is for life, not just for Christmas. There are other birds, and beasts (oh yes, and vegetarian options), which the family might like better. Very few children like Brussels sprouts. And virtually no children like figgy pudding. Food at Christmas should be something people actually like, rather than feel they have a duty to sweat through! It's the same with the drink: unless the family actually *likes* mulled wine, it's not compulsory. Moreover these days not many people enjoy over-eating, and they might be much happier and less inclined to quarrel over the party games if they don't feel quite ill after too much stuffing and cheap bubbly. In a curious way, the English seem to have devised a way of feasting that is actually a penance rather than a joy.

Christmas should be a joy. So in choosing what to eat and drink, the criterion should be what you enjoy cooking and eating, and what will leave you feeling happy rather than bloated: and never mind what the neighbours say! The point is to be happy: our Catholic faith is actually meant to make us happy, and the good things God has given us are for our enjoyment.

Hospitality and charity

Enjoyment does include sharing, so that charity and hospitality are very important parts of our celebration. During the Twelve Days of Christmas there will be opportunities for entertaining friends and family, and perhaps also strangers and former enemies. We should be lavish in our entertainment: but we should also remember the poor, and try to give something in proportion to what we spend on ourselves. "Whatsoever you do to the least of my brethren, you do unto Me."

Christ at the centre

Christ must be the centre of our Christmas, so that prayer and the celebration of Mass are absolutely essential. Many people love Midnight Mass and churches are often so crowded that a second sitting has to be provided, rather earlier (and therefore perhaps more suitable for the little ones). But it seems a shame to go to Mass on the Eve and not on the day itself. The dawn Mass in many ways is the loveliest, on a crisp winter morning with a hint of frost. But the Mass is what Christ-Mass is all about: the actual present coming of Jesus Christ into our midst. The holidays can all be holy days if we go to daily Mass, rejoicing in the saints, and the different aspects of the Incarnation expressed in the liturgy.

Eucharist and Prayer

If we live too far from the church for daily Mass, we can still mark the feasts in our family prayer, reading some of the prayers and texts of the Mass, and praying on St Stephen's day for those being persecuted; on Innocents' Day for the unborn; on St John's day for evangelists; on St Thomas' day for bishops, and so on. Our meals should begin with prayer, and these special days can be marked with different forms from those we normally use. Night and morning prayers can also be subtly different to mark the different moods of the liturgy: we can use parts of the Divine Office together even if we have no opportunity for the whole of it. Prayer thrives on routine, and it is all too easy to neglect prayer during holiday time when routine breaks down, so we shall need to make a special effort to pray in special ways on these special days.

Christmas is the season to be jolly: and jollity begins with the love of God, made flesh in the love of each other.

THE CHRISTMAS SAINTS

The three great saints' days after Christmas have been observed since the time of the earliest calendars of which we have records. St Stephen on 26 December, St John the Evangelist on 27 December and the Holy Innocents on 29 December have been kept since the days before the Roman emperor liberated the Church, the time of the Roman Martyrs. We shall probably never know how these dates came to be fixed, but we know enough to set us thinking how we should now observe these feasts and benefit by the spirit of the liturgy.

St Stephen - 26 December

St Stephen is not part of the Christmas story. It is just possible that 26 December, the day after Christmas, was, or was thought to be, the historic anniversary of his death, but this does not seem particularly likely. We know, however, that apart from great gospel events like the Ascension of Christ, the earliest occasions for weekday festivals were the anniversaries of the martyrs. We also believe that in the period before the season of Advent was instituted, Christmas was the beginning of the Church's year. During the period of the persecutions, the martyrs were the most important of the saints - much more important than they now seem to us. This was because martyrs were perfectly united with Christ in their lives and in their deaths. Without the martyrs there would have been no faith and no Church. It would be reasonable for the Church to want to remember Stephen, the first and greatest of Martyrs, on the second day of the year, immediately after the feast of Christmas, the first possible day for celebrating any martyr.

Christ had himself taught about the importance of martyrdom, both when he reminded the disciples that they must be ready to give up their lives for him, and whenever he taught them to witness to the faith. He promised salvation to those who endure to the end. A new Christian may face an early death, perhaps with violent suffering; or endure many years of temptation. One way or another every Christian has to be a martyr.

This means that a martyr is saint for everybody, because all must be martyrs. By remembering Stephen on the day after Christmas we commit ourselves to faithful witness for the faith. Martyrs are not just Catholic saints; they are Gospel saints.

Notice how clearly the story of St Stephen in Acts 2 encourages us to faithful witness, and to bearing our vocation with confidence. Jesus stands by the dying Stephen and inspires him to die in union with himself - a Christlike death in which he closely imitates his Lord, from the prayer for his persecutors to the prayer from

Psalm130 entrusting his dying soul into his Father's hands, 'Into thy hands, O Lord I commend my spirit...'

St John the Evangelist - 27 December

St John the Evangelist does not tell the Christmas story in his Gospel. Celebrating him on 27 December turns our attention to the content the Gospel, that Jesus brought to the world and St John's gospel gives the most personal and graphic account of the reality of the manhood that God assumed in Jesus. Here is the core and origin of the Christian religion. Possessing the Gospel is the greatest joy in the world, taking up into itself all other joys, the sharing of Christ's own life. John is not only the evangelist who insists most firmly that he has touched Jesus in the flesh as well as spoken with him. John is also the strongest human witness for the Incarnation of the Son of God in Jesus. John records the words, 'I am the way' and 'I am the Bread of life, and 'I am the vine, you are the branches.' More than the other gospels he emphasises our spiritual union with Jesus, showing us in Chapter 6 that God is truly present in Word and Sacrament. If Stephen shows how to live and die for Christ, then St John teaches how to know Christ and to draw strength from him for our duty of witness. This is something for which we are indebted to the Evangelists, not least to John. Every Christian is a witness, and all Christians depend on the apostles and evangelists. In celebrating St John we are led to think about the essence of our faith and how we have received it, in a way that rounds out the understanding of witness we found in celebrating St Stephen.

God gives us the Gospel in book form because we cannot receive it in any other way, and because of its content the gospel is the Book of Books, actually bringing Christ to us, so that we can know him as well as any other person we love. More than that, we can grow like him. Notice that the Gospel does not teach us that Jesus is good and kind to people - that would be a watered down version of the Good News. The scriptures show us Christ being firm and making people face harsh choices, as well as comforting and helping them. They show him living and dying for the human race. There is no difference between the 'Christ of History' and the 'Christ of Theology'. We cannot simply learn about him and try to copy him. St John above all says we must become one with him. Christ does more than rescue us; he empowers us.

For the same reason, we begin reading St John's letters at mass today.

The Gospel Reading shows us St John when he receives the news of the Resurrection, the crown of the life whose beginning we celebrate at Christmas.

Feast of the Holy Innocents - 28 December

When we come to the Holy Innocents on 28 December, we enter another way of thinking about the Christmas

calendar. They are an historical part of the Christmas
story and give us a festival of a different kind. This feast,
like Christmas day itself, commemorates an event, the sad
story of the murdered baby boys. This is the closing
incident of the Christmas story in St Matthew's Gospel,
and finishes the Bethlehem story; but the story is
disordered in the ancient liturgical calendar, because the
visit of the wise men is separated from the story of the
innocents, and placed on 6 January, where it becomes a
festival of light. It is actually better for us to separate the
historical tragedy and remember it together with the
celebration of the Incarnation.

The Christmas Octave - 8 days

In Christmas week (more accurately called the Christmas
Octave or 'eight days'), we also keep two more saints'
days, keeping them in the simplest way possible, lest they
overshadow the Christmas festivities: St Sylvester and St
Thomas Becket. They are important enough to be kept on
their anniversary days though they have no special
spiritual connection with Christmas. St Sylvester was
pope, or Bishop of Rome, when the Emperor Constantine
made Christianity the official religion of the whole
Roman Empire. He is part of the history of the whole
Church, and is celebrated throughout the world. St
Thomas Becket is remembered by priests everywhere
because he is patron saint of the clergy, but he is

especially remembered in England because he was archbishop of Canterbury. He was martyred in Canterbury Cathedral on 29 December, defending the Church's freedom in the course of a long and bitter quarrel between the King and the Church.

The Feast of the Holy Family - Sunday of Octave

The Feast of the Holy Family is kept on the Sunday in the Christmas Octave, or, if Christmas day is itself a Sunday, on Friday 30 December. It takes up the Bethlehem picture of Jesus, Mary and Joseph, so that we give our attention to the way in which they lived together and so helps us in our own family life.

People who live alone or in one-parent families should not let themselves feel hurt or discouraged on this day. Whatever the reason why some parents and children do not live together, that reason is never that God loves some of us less than others. Two things need to be remembered. Jesus, Mary and Joseph have the same relationship to all Christians. As Jesus himself said, we who believe in him are all his brothers and sisters and we can all rely on receiving the same help from him. Nevertheless those of us who live in a complete human family should spend a little time every Christmas in praying for those who have an incomplete family or no family at all.

Parentage is a vocation, a call from God (Year A)

The Gospel Reading gives the same event from two different angles. Each of the two stories tells of the angel giving Joseph a message, and then quoting the Old Testament. In the first story the angel tells Joseph to take the little boy to Egypt for safety; and refers to a simple, direct message about the Son of God being taken as a refugee in Egypt. The quotation is from Hosea. In the second story the angel tells Joseph to take Jesus back to Israel when there is no further danger from Herod; and the Old Testament reference says the boy will become a man of Nazareth, even though he was not born there. This reference, however, is not a specific text from any particular place in the Bible.

The Father's care for his beloved people Israel is one with his care for his divine Son. Nazareth stands for the nation. Notice how little the Bible tells us about Jesus and Nazareth. He was not born there, and did little preaching or miracle-working there. It was the place where he lived unnoticed until his 'hour' came. The life of the Holy Family was not a fairy-tale life. It was lived against the background of King Herod's wickedness and the hated Roman occupation. It was almost certainly lived in an 'extended family', with all the tensions of many relations living closely together in one establishment. There is a hint of this in Mark 3:31. The holiness of the Holy Family lay in the lives of Jesus, Mary and Joseph living in the ordinary world, where God dwelt in them all.

The duty of respect of father and mother, and the sanctification of parenthood (Year B)

The readings first show us God giving Isaac as a child of promise to Abraham, the heir of his own flesh and blood, through whom Abraham would live for ever; and second Abraham's willingness to return that great gift to God. The Gospel Reading tells the story of Mary and Joseph offering the baby Jesus in the Temple, in the same spirit of obedience as Abraham offered Isaac.

A holy family life is all giving (Year C)

The New Testament letter belongs with the Christmas-time readings from the letters of St John.

The Gospel Reading is about the incident in Jerusalem when Jesus was 12 years old. It is important not to get drawn into useless speculations as to whether Jesus was a naughty boy or Joseph was careless. We simply do not know enough about family customs of the time to be able to say anything about this sort of detail. It is better to see what ideas may have been in the Evangelist's mind as he presented this record.

Twelve years old was nearing the time when a boy might be thinking of marriage and entering adulthood. (We all know that Jewish boys today have the 'Bar Mitzvah' at about this age.) This story then, marks the end of his childhood. The Temple has a special place in St

Luke's Gospel, especially at the beginning and end. God had given the temple to Israel, and it would not be needed after its veil was destroyed at the crucifixion. This is a mid-point. When he comes to the Temple on the night of his trial he will be questioned again by learned men. When he is twelve they know nothing about him; when he is 33 they will have heard his Gospel and must make their choice. This story is another linking of the life of the Holy Family with the Good News.

Solemnity of Mary, Mother of God

After the Vatican Council the Church no longer called this day 'The circumcision', nor even the 'The name of Jesus', but found a way of sealing the octave of Christmas that is highly theological and warmly devotional, but rooted in ancient liturgical tradition and has some relevance to the fact that for most of the world this is the civil New Year's Day. The Church goes back, then, to the earliest record we have of celebrating this day in the city of Rome with what was then the first and only commemoration of the Motherhood of Mary. Her motherhood is the source for all liturgical celebrations of our Lady, a wonderful basis for feasts of the whole year.

One of the ancient Roman antiphons, still used today at Vespers, is:

"O wonderful exchange! The Creator of human nature took on a human body and was born of the Virgin. He became man without having a human father and has bestowed on us his divine nature."

Another is:

"You were born of the Virgin in a mysterious manner of which no man can speak; you fulfilled the scriptures: like rain falling gently on the earth you came hither to save the human race. We praise you; you are our God."

At first sight the Old Testament reading may seem puzzling. It is a blessing which Aaron as chief of priests is to give to all the people. It mentions neither Our Lady nor the time of year. One way of unlocking this message is to recall the words of John 3:27 about Christ bringing us peace, and Ephesians 2:14-15. In the Incarnation, Christ 'uncovers his face' and brings us peace. This prayer asks us to praise God as he blesses us with peace 'not as this world gives peace'. The blend of thanksgiving and prayer for blessings is exactly what we need on New Year's Day.

Psalm 66 uses the idea of the prophecy from Numbers to make a song.

The New Testament Reading from Galatians is a basic statement of the Incarnation, cast in Trinitarian form and explicitly mentioning the woman who becomes the Mother of God.

The Gospel Reading gives us all that St Luke says about the birth at Bethlehem. It will have been heard by those who were at the Dawn Mass on Christmas day, but adds the details of what happened on the eighth day.

Epiphany

The Solemnity of the Epiphany is celebrated in the Western Catholic Church on or around the 6th January, which is twelve days after the Solemnity of Christmas. A Solemnity is a celebration of the most significant aspects of our faith. Feast days and memorials also celebrate important people and events and 'Feast' is often used as a general term to refer to any of these. Epiphany means 'manifestation' or 'showing' and this is what is celebrated, though it encompasses a wider range of events than the revealing of the Son of God to the Wise Men, which is what we now focus on for the most part.

History

From the early days of the Church, the celebrating of the Epiphany of the Lord has been linked with the birth of Jesus. In the beginning these celebrations focused mainly on the revelatory aspect of the Nativity, the showing of the infant Jesus to the shepherds. (The Church was not eager to commemorate Christ's birthday as such to begin with, as it was a pagan custom to celebrate the birthdays of the gods.) There is evidence of Epiphany being celebrated in third century Egypt where it is linked to another manifestation of Christ - his baptism in the Jordan. The Baptism of Christ seems to have been the event most often celebrated at Epiphany, but the manifestation of Christ at the Wedding Feast in Cana was also connected to this very early on, as was the coming of the Wise Men. Nowadays, although the Mass for the Solemnity focuses exclusively on the coming of the Magi and their adoration of Christ the infant King, the Breviary has many references to the two other manifestations.

The Western Church took up the Feast of the Epiphany a little later than the Eastern and celebrated it as a separate feast from Christmas. It quickly became associated with three main manifestations of Christ; to the Wise Men, at his Baptism and at the Wedding in Cana. Gradually more importance became attached to the appearing of the Wise Men.

Manifestation to the Wise Men

St. Matthew is the only one of the Gospel writers to tell us of this event.

"Now when Jesus was born in Bethlehem of Judea in the days of Herod the king, behold, wise men from the East came to Jerusalem, saying, "Where is he who has been born king of the Jews? For we have seen his star in the East, and have come to worship him... and lo, the star which they had seen in the East went before them, till it came to rest over the place where the child was. When they saw the star, they rejoiced exceedingly with great joy; and going into the house they saw the child with

Mary his mother, and they fell down and worshiped him. Then, opening their treasures, they offered him gifts, gold and frankincense and myrrh. And being warned in a dream not to return to Herod, they departed to their own country by another way." (*Mt* 2:1-12).

St. Matthew calls the Wise Men Magi; from this word we derive our 'magic' and 'magician'. The Wise Men were unlikely to have been practitioners of magic as we understand it though. They probably came from Persia, from the sacred class of the Medes, and were priests of a religion rather like Zoroastrianism. This religion forbade the use of sorcery, but would have enabled them to develop an interest in Astrology and the interpretation of dreams. They have sometimes been thought of and referred to as 'the three kings', though there is nothing to suggest this in the Gospel account except the reference to 'treasures' which implies, at least, that they were well off. Another probable source of their supposed kingship are various Old Testament passages which have been used in the Church's worship at this feast, and which have been taken as referring literally, rather than liturgically, to the event. For example: "And nations shall come to your light, and kings to the brightness of your rising." (*Is* 60:3)

Neither is there anything to indicate the number of Magi who made the journey to Bethlehem; the number three seems to have become established because of the three gifts mentioned, or possibly even because it was thought a fitting and auspicious number. However, there are traditions and works of art which suggest different numbers; two, four, eight or even twelve.

By the seventh century, and possibly earlier, we find that the Magi have acquired names which are usually some form of Caspar, Melchior and Balthasar, though Eastern Churches have different names for them. Traditions built up which linked each 'king' with a particular country or race and many popular customs and stories developed to reflect this. Various interpretations have also been given to the gifts themselves; gold is said to be a fit gift for a King (though it would also have been very useful for a poor family who had to flee to Egypt shortly), incense indicates both the divinity and priesthood of Christ, and myrrh foreshadows his death.

The star which guided the Magi has been attributed to various origins. It was perhaps a conjunction of planets, or a supernova or a comet, but whatever it was, it was observed by the Magi and accounted as of great significance. The preparations and journey from the 'East' - perhaps Persia (present day Iran) or Babylonia (now Southern Iraq) would have taken at least several months, so it is likely that the infant Jesus was an older baby, or even a toddler at the time of their arrival. King Herod's order to kill all the male children of two years old or less certainly indicates that some considerable time had passed.

To understand this Epiphany, we have to look both ways - at Jesus Christ and at the Magi. The child Jesus was born to humble parents in a rather insignificant corner of the Roman Empire which was troubled, then as now, by political unrest. Yet this child was God the Son, the second person of the Holy Trinity, and the whole of creation was made through him. If we are looking for a king on this occasion, we must be sure to look the right way. Christ the King chose these parents, this place, and these men to whom he would manifest himself. Christ, who is the light of the world, shone forth in that obscure place and revealed his glory by the light of a star.

We can find much significance in the Magi themselves. As non-Jews, they represent the whole of humanity in all its racial variety, showing us that Christ has come to redeem the whole world, not only the Jewish race. Their gifts can be understood as representing every aspect of human life - material riches, spirituality, and death - though they themselves need not have been aware of this. They have been guided by a heavenly light to the Light of Heaven himself and acknowledge the Messiah-King whom his own people would reject.

Manifestation at his Baptism

This event is recorded in all four Gospels. (*Mt* 3:13-17; *Mk* 1:9-11; *Lk* 3:21-22; *Jn* 1:29-34) and is recalled as soon as Christmastide has closed.

"In those days Jesus came from Nazareth of Galilee and was baptized by John in the Jordan. And when he came up out of the water, immediately he saw the heavens opened and the Spirit descending upon him like a dove; and a voice came from heaven, "Thou art my beloved Son; with thee I am well pleased." (*Mk* 1:9-11).

The manifestation of Christ's glory as the Son of the Father became a matter for greater public awareness at this point. No longer hidden in a humble lodging at Bethlehem, Jesus is now observed by the crowds who had come to be baptised by John. The *Catechism of the Catholic Church* tells us that, "The baptism of Jesus is on his part the acceptance and inauguration of his mission as God's suffering Servant. He allows himself to be numbered among sinners; he is already "the Lamb of God, who takes away the sin of the world". Already he is anticipating the "baptism" of his bloody death. Already he is coming to "fulfil all righteousness", that is, he is submitting himself entirely to his Father's will: out of love he consents to this baptism of death for the remission of our sins" (*CCC*, 536). The baptism of Jesus inaugurates a new beginning for the world - as the Holy Spirit moved upon the face of the waters at the creation, so now we find the Holy Spirit, in the form of a dove, hovering over the waters where Jesus begins the redemptive work which will recreate us.

The event is clearly and specifically Trinitarian; Jesus the Son receives a visible manifestation of the Holy Spirit in the form of a dove, and an audible manifestation of the Father's love. The manifestation of the Spirit is given also to John the Baptist who will be the witness of the event and perhaps to the watching crowds as well. In this event Jesus is revealed as the Christ whose mission is to baptise believers with the Holy Spirit, thereby enabling them to share the fire of his divine life. In contemplating this event, we find a glimpse of the Trinitarian life of God himself manifested to us - we learn not only that Jesus is God, but also that God is himself a communion of love.

Manifestation at the wedding feast

Only St. John gives us an account of this event. This is commemorated on the Sunday following the Baptism of the Lord.

"On the third day there was a marriage at Cana in Galilee, and the mother of Jesus was there; Jesus also was invited to the marriage, with his disciples. When the wine failed, the mother of Jesus said to him, "They have no wine." And Jesus said to her, "O woman, what have you to do with me? My hour has not yet come." His mother said to the servants, "Do whatever he tells you."

"Now six stone jars were standing there, for the Jewish rites of purification, each holding twenty or thirty gallons. Jesus said to them, "Fill the jars with water." And they filled them up to the brim. He said to them, "Now draw some out, and take it to the steward of the feast." So they took it. When the steward of the feast tasted the water now become wine, and did not know where it came from (though the servants who had drawn the water knew), the steward of the feast called the bridegroom and said to him, "Every man serves the good wine first; and when men have drunk freely, then the poor wine; but you have kept the good wine until now." This, the first of his signs, Jesus did at Cana in Galilee, and manifested his glory; and his disciples believed in him." (*Jn* 2:1-11).

Here we find that Jesus, in revealing his glory, also reveals his power and his mission, though both are still veiled in some way. Mary his Mother and the disciples knew what had happened, and the servants knew. The steward, the bridegroom and probably the main body of the guests were unaware of what had taken place - Jesus' power was only manifested to those he trusted, or who seemed insignificant. Jesus' mission, which is to lift us from the poverty of our fallen existence and raise us to the glorious life of God himself, is not yet manifested as such. However, the transformation of water, which is the drink of the poor, to wine, which is drunk by those who are rich, or who are joyfully celebrating, provides us with a valuable symbolism. The wine itself is symbolic of the messianic wedding festivities foretold in the Old Testament. Jesus' glory as Son of the Father and Saviour of the world is manifested for those who have eyes to see and who believe in him.

These three 'epiphanies' are linked in that they reveal the glory of Christ to those he has chosen, those who need to believe in him and those who already do. They require both faith and action from those who understand, at least in part, what they are seeing. Once received, the manifestation of his glory cannot be ignored. We must, as Mary asks, do whatever he tells us.

Celebrating the Feast of the Epiphany

In many homes Epiphany, or Twelfth Night, marks the end of the Christmas festivities. The tree and decorations are taken down and packed away for another year and life resumes as normal. However, the Crib need not disappear so soon, especially if the Wise Men have only just arrived. Many families like to place the Wise Men figures in another part of the room over Christmas, or even somewhere else in the house, and have them travel a little further each day until they arrive at the Crib for Epiphany. It can be a good idea to keep them there until the three Epiphany events have been celebrated, or even until Candlemas - the end of the old 'long Christmas' season.

A custom which marks a beginning at this season rather than an ending is the Blessing of the Kings. In its simplest form, this consists of a prayer asking God's blessing on the home and the marking of the following on the lintel above the door with chalk, preferably blessed previously.

20+C+M+B+07

The numbers represent the year and the letters are the supposed initials of the Wise Men, Caspar, Melchior and Balthasar. CMB also stands for *Christus Mansionem Benedicat* - Christ bless this house. Children may like to have a procession to the door, holy water may be used, Scripture may be read and hymns sung to enrich the celebration.

Prayer for the Blessing of the Kings

Lord God of heaven and earth,
you have given us your only Son.
You showed him to the Wise Men at Bethlehem
by the light of a star:
You revealed him to John the Baptist
    by the river Jordan
and you made known his love and power at the
    wedding in Cana.
Bless this, our home;
bless all who come in through this door
    and all who leave.
Let the light of Christ fill our lives
and let our love for others reflect your love for us.
We ask this through Jesus Christ, our Lord. Amen.

40 DAYS OF CHRISTMAS?

Christmas was doubtless originally a one-day celebration, but there must have been a very early impulse to extend mid-winter merry-making, if nothing more, that led Christians to feel that one day was not enough. The idea of keeping a feast up for a week eventually crystallised into the mediaeval custom of continuing any great feast into an 'octave' of 8 days. By the 20th century the Calendar was cluttered with too many octaves. So in 1970 they were cut down to just two: Easter and Christmas. We have seen in the earlier parts of this booklet, how the Church extends its bible-readings and meditations on the Incarnation into the Christmas Octave.

We have also seen how in the Liturgy, the atmosphere and subject matter of Christmas are linked with Epiphany. This lengthens Christmas to 12 days, and many people still keep their Christmas decorations up until the 12thh night. Shakespeare's 'Twelfth Night' was a play for this occasion, the official end of Christmas parties.

The Church marks the twelfth night as the feast of the Epiphany, which spiritually deepens and extends our understanding of the Christmas mystery. We now celebrate Epiphany until the feast of the Lord's Baptism, which occurs within a week of Epiphany.

This brings us again to the distinction between festivals that commemorate events in the Bible story and the celebrations of great Christian themes, such as Trinity Sunday always has been and Epiphany originally was. We also run again into spoiling of the chronological order of the celebrations (We have already seen how the Holy Innocents and the Epiphany have become dislocated). This is because when the Church commemorates the presentation of the Child Jesus in the Temple on 2 February, because St Luke says the presentation took place when the Lord was 40 days old, our mind are taken back six weeks to Christmas day, though the Sunday Readings have moved on to the wedding in Cana, when Christ is fully adult. Some noticed the parallel with the 40 days of Lent and even spoke of 'Forty days of Christmas'. The same idea re-appeared from time to time in other ways. In France during the 19th century, for instance, it was quite common to have special devotions to the Childhood of Jesus throughout January, much as devotions to our Lady flourished in May, to the Sacred Heart of Jesus in June, and to the Precious Blood in July.

Devotions to the Holy Childhood throughout January must now be extremely rare, since the Church has succeeded now in restoring the liturgical reading of Scripture to its central place in the prayers of the laity. Before 1970 the Sunday Gospel Readings used to relate in a gentle fashion to the Christmas - Epiphany readings. Epiphany led us from the historical Incarnation of the Son of God at Christmas, to his manifestation to the world and the powerful working of his grace in all creation, which was the theme of the Sunday Gospel readings between Epiphany and Septuagesima Sunday of the pre-Conciliar liturgy. In our present lectionary there is an underlying structure that is fundamentally similar: the Ordinary Sundays of the year begin reading the Gospel with Jesus preaching and working miracles in Galilee - the very period of the manifestation of God in Christ that characterised the same Sundays in the former lectionary.

So we shall find ourselves hearing the Gospel read to us in a meaningful order that began way back before Christmas in the prophetic readings of Advent.

Informative Catholic Reading

We hope that you have enjoyed reading this booklet.

If you would like to find out more about CTS booklets - we'll send you our free information pack and catalogue.

Please send us your details:

Name ....

Address ....

....

....

Postcode ....

Telephone ....

Email ....

Send to: CTS, 40-46 Harleyford Road,
           Vauxhall, London
           SE11 5AY

Tel: 020 7640 0042
Fax: 020 7640 0046
Email: info@cts-online.org.uk